Birgit]

Lay the table

- with Bobbin Lace

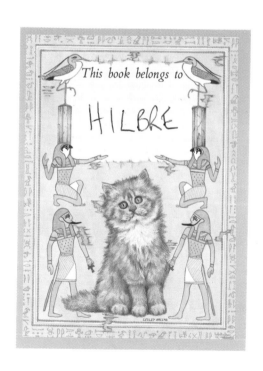

This book belongs to

HILBRE

Akacia

Forlaget Akacia
Skovvænget 1
DK - 5690 Tommerup
akacia@akacia.dk

Printed at Øko-Tryk I/S, Videbæk, Denmark, 2002

ISBN: 87-7847-047-1

Foreword

It has been exiting and interesting to work on this book, where the theme, as the title says, has been lace for the table. I have designed lace for both practical use and simply for decoration.

I have chosen to use colours in this lace, with either white or unbleached thread for the background colour, as it gives a very delicate effect. I would recommend Goldschild linen thread, because this 3-ply thread is really lovely to work with and it gives a nice result.

Twists are indicated on the diagrams where I think they are needed, but feel free to add twists as you find appropriate when you work these patterns.

A big thank you to Inge Lindegaard. She has given plenty of good advice, lots of ideas and great support throughout the whole process of making this book. Also thanks to my husband Poul-Erik, who needed great patience during the making of this book.

I hope you will all enjoy this book.

Birgit Poulsen

Contents

Placemat "Hearts"

Materials:
17 pairs Goldschild linen Nel 80/3
1 red pair Goldschild linen Nel 80/3 for every heart
1 pair ground colour Goldschild linen Nel 80/3, to be used after the heart is finished (to replace the red pair).

Instructions:
Start at the point with 4 pairs, see fig. 1. Add pairs along the diagonal plait, one pair at every pin as shown by the arrows in figs. 2a and 2b. The pair and plait meet as shown in fig. 3. At the beginning of the heart, one ground colour pair is replaced by a red pair, see fig. 4, and the reverse at the end of the heart, fig. 5.

To finish:
At the end of the lace, the pairs are worked into the plait and are „thrown out", see fig. 6. It is important to work to this point before throwing out, to make sure the threads are secure.
The lace is stitched onto the left corner of the placemat.

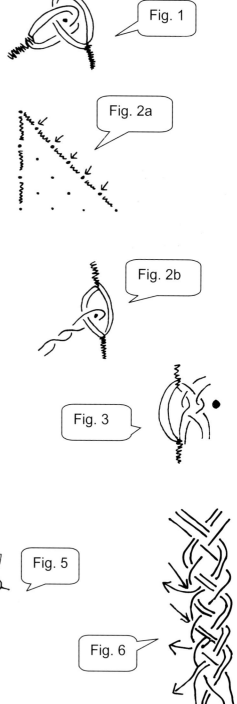

Fig. 1

Fig. 2a

Fig. 2b

Fig. 3

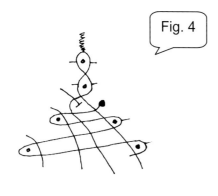

Fig. 4

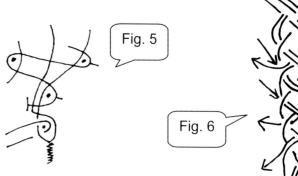

Fig. 5

Fig. 6

Placemat "Hearts"

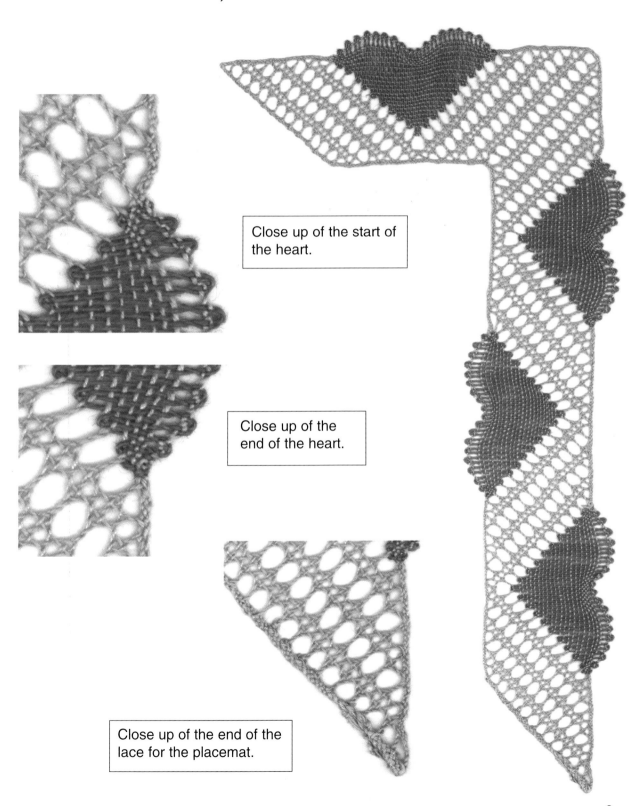

Close up of the start of the heart.

Close up of the end of the heart.

Close up of the end of the lace for the placemat.

Placemat "Hearts"

Placemat "Hearts"

Serviette ring "Hearts"

Materials:

8 pairs Goldschild linen Nel 50/3 ground colour
1 pair Goldschild linen Nel 50/3 heart colour

Instructions:

Start and work as shown in the diagram. Add the heart pair as shown in fig. 1 and remove it as in fig. 2 (page 13). At the ⊢ sign, the pair is laid back and then cut off when the lace is finished.

To finish:

The work ends with a „linen finish" as shown in the diagram. (See „Techniques," page 79.) The last 2 pairs are plaited and can make a loop for a button fastening or have a press stud sewn onto each end.

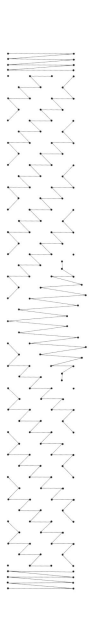

12

Serviette ring "Hearts"

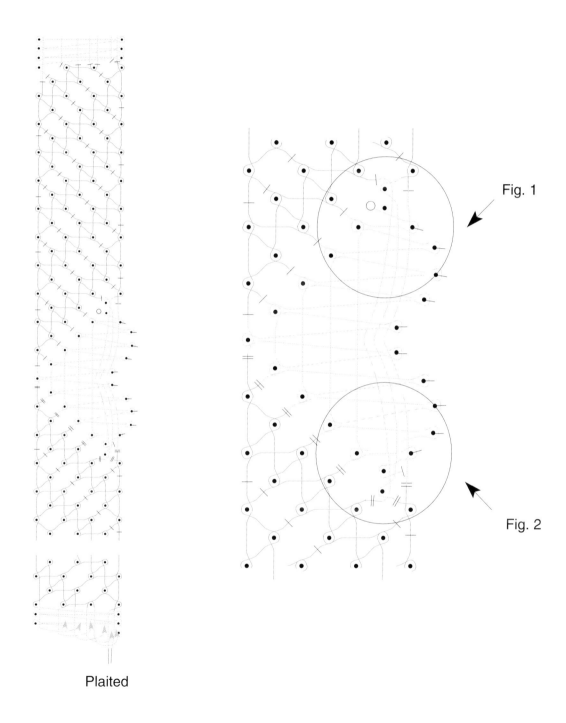

Fig. 1

Fig. 2

Plaited

Candlestick decoration "Hearts"

Materials:

10 pairs Goldschild linen Nel 50/3 ground colour
1 pair Goldschild linen Nel 50/3 heart colour

Instructions:

Set on and work as shown in the diagram. Add the heart worker pair at #. The workers and other pairs meet the plait as shown in fig. 1.

To finish:

Sew out into the start of the lace and make secure by „Tying off with knots," see p.79, or any finishing technique you prefer

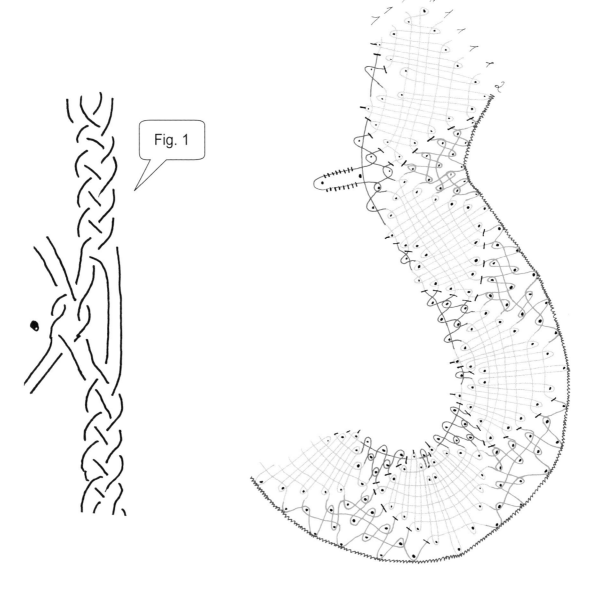

Fig. 1

Candlestick decoration "Hearts"

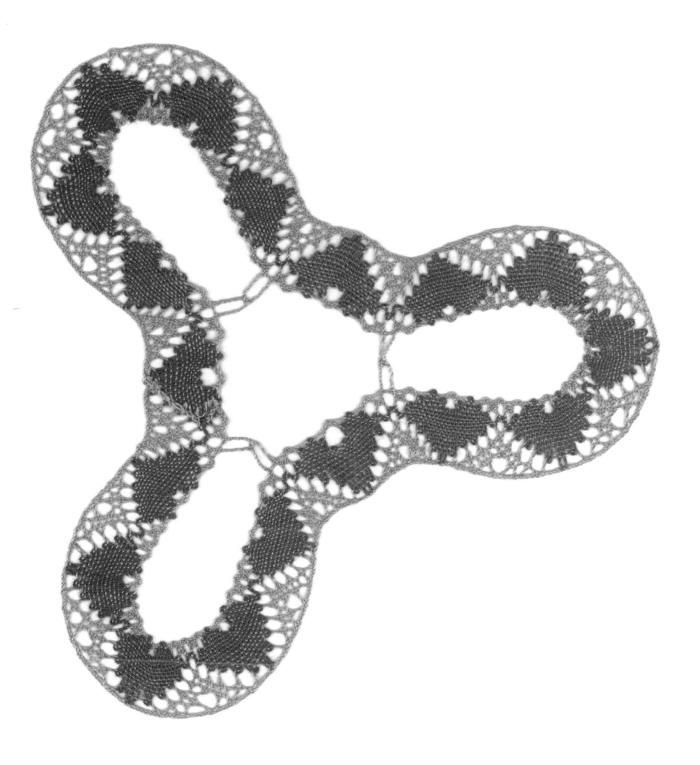

Placemat "Tulip"

Materials:

20 pairs Goldschild linen Nel 50/3 ground colour
1 pair Goldschild linen Nel 50/3 tulip colour. Fill
one bobbin and wind 1m onto its partner.

Instructions:

Work on the reverse side. Start at the point as shown
in fig. 1 and add new pairs along the diagonal (fig.
2). Follow the diagram on p.21. The purple workers
are added as shown in fig. 3 and taken out as in fig.
4. (The pair is laid back and then cut off when the
lace is finished.) When the first tulip is finished and
the pair has been cut off, wind 1 m onto the „empty"
bobbin. It is important that the purple pair is pulled
tight at the end of every row, but no so tight that
the pattern becomes distorted.

To finish:

The lace also finishes on the diagonal, leaving out
pairs as shown in fig. 5. (Pairs are laid back when
you get to ⊣ and then cut off when the lace is
finished.) The point is completed as shown in fig. 6.
When you get to position A, tie a knot with one
thread from each pair twice. Repeat at B. When you
get to the point, turn your pillow round and plait
back over top of the work. The threads tied at B
and A will then be tied over the plait to hold it in
place. It is important to shape the point as neatly as
possible.

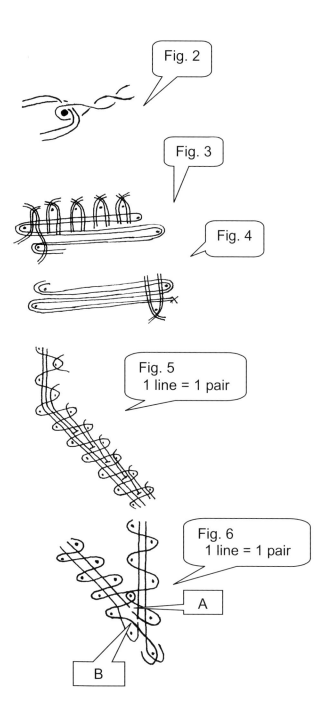

Fig. 2

Fig. 3

Fig. 4

Fig. 5
1 line = 1 pair

Fig. 6
1 line = 1 pair

A

B

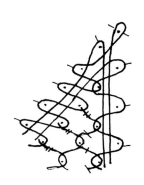

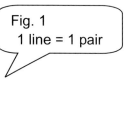

Fig. 1
1 line = 1 pair

Placemat "Tulip"

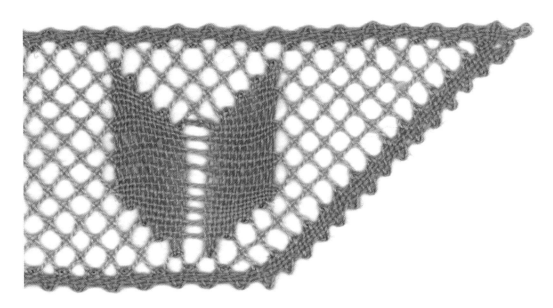

Close up of the start
of the tulip placemat

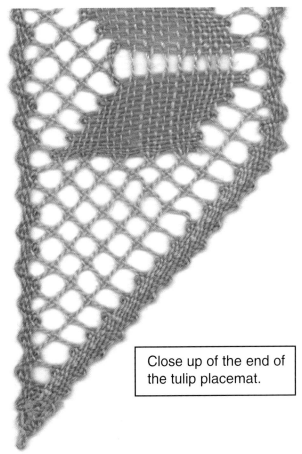

Close up of the end of
the tulip placemat.

Placemat "Tulip"

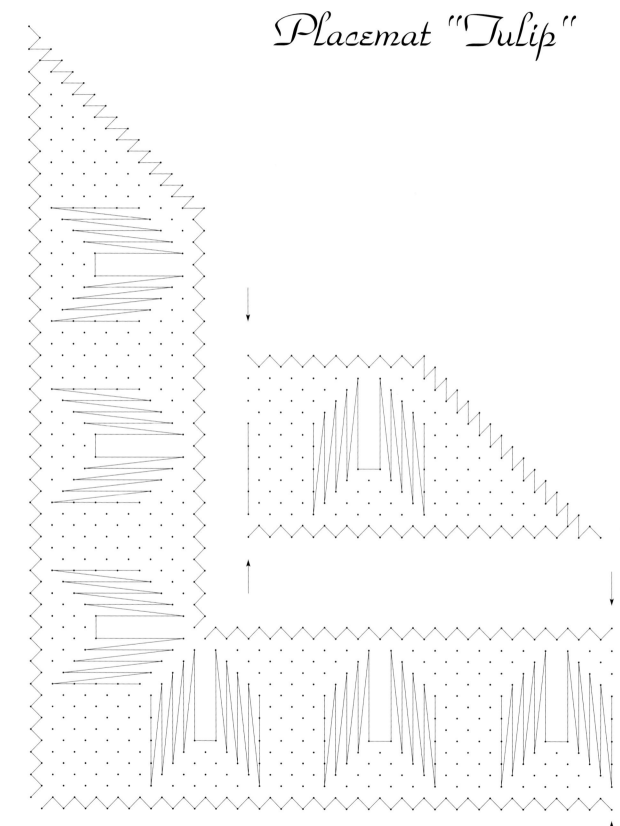

Placemat "Tulip"

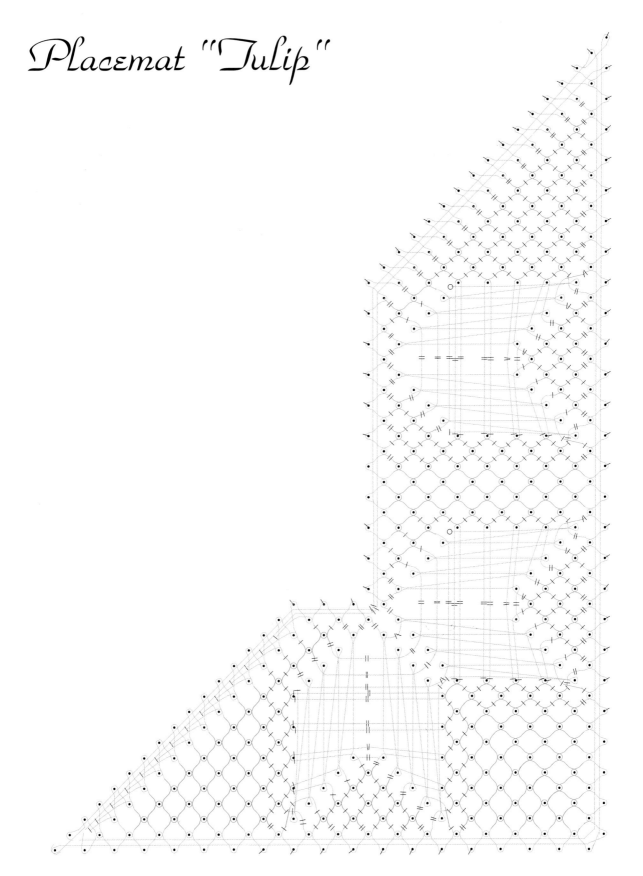

Placemat
"Tulip"

Serviette ring
"Tulip"

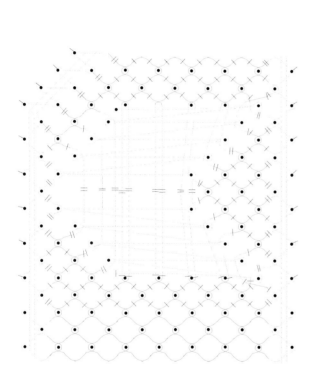

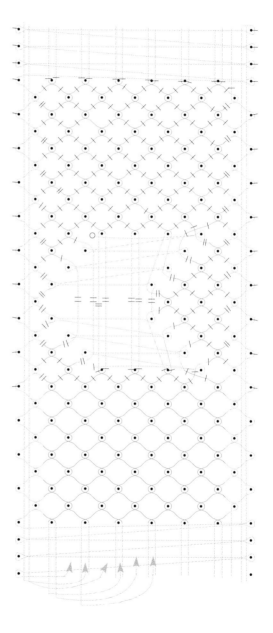

Serviette ring "Tulip"

Materials:
12 pairs Goldschild linen Nel 50/3 ground colour
7 pairs Goldschild linen Nel 50/3 tulip colour

Instructions:
Set on and work as shown in the diagram.

To finish:
Work a linen finish as the diagram shows. (See
p.79) The last 2 pairs are plaited and can make a
loop for a button fastening or have a press stud
sewn onto each end.

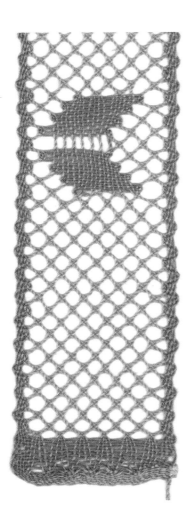

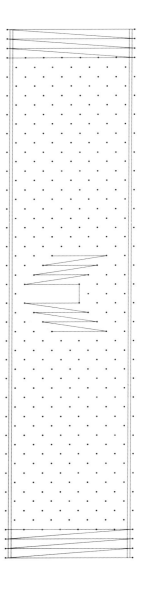

Candlestick decoration "Tulip"

Materials:

The ring:

10 pairs Goldschild linen Nel 50/3 ground colour

2 pairs Goldschild linen Nel 50/3 tulip colour

2 pairs Goldschild linen Nel 50/3 leaf colour

The tulip tape:

10 pairs Goldschild linen Nel 50/3 ground colour

2 pairs Goldschild linen Nel 50/3 tulip colour

Instructions:

The ring with green tape:

* shows where the tulip colour workers begin. Set on and work as shown in the diagram. At the outer edge, the ground colour pair and the tulip colour pair work (CTTC) as fig. 1, to keep the colours in place.

The green tape:

The colours must be set on in the correct order. The two ground colour pairs will be passives, one at each side. One green pair is placed in the middle: the other is the worker pair.

The tulip tape:

Set on and work a shown in the diagram. Finish with a 2 rows of cloth stitch and a linen finish. (See p.79.)

To make up:

Make 3 tulip tapes and stitch them to the wrong side of the ring.

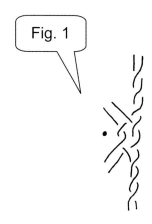

Fig. 1

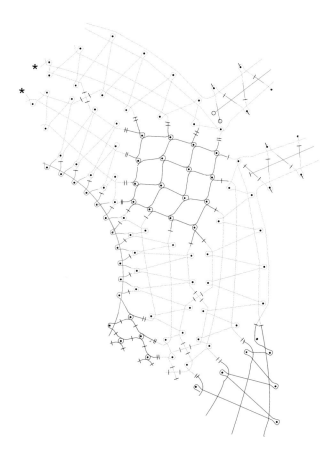

24

Candlestick decoration "Tulip"

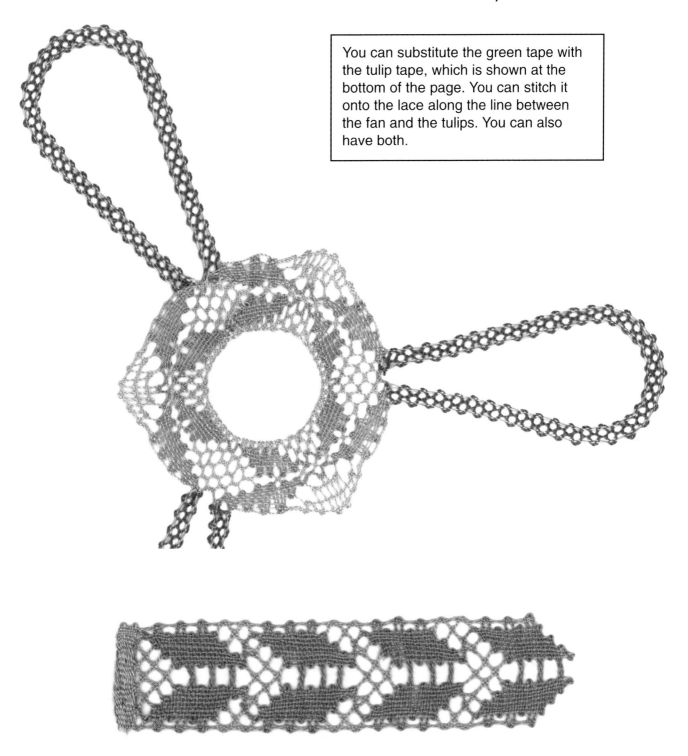

You can substitute the green tape with the tulip tape, which is shown at the bottom of the page. You can stitch it onto the lace along the line between the fan and the tulips. You can also have both.

Candlestick decoration "Tulip"

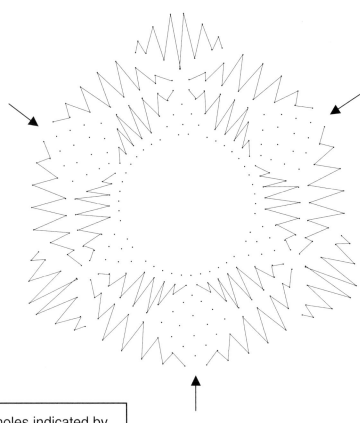

The row of pinholes indicated by the arrows is printed on both sections of the pricking, so they must overlap.

Candlestick decoration "Tulip"

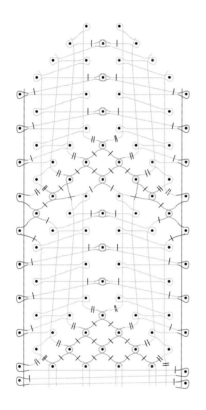

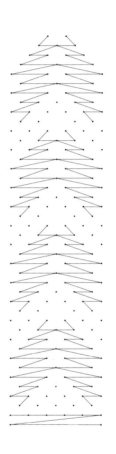

Never ending doilies

Materials:
Cockle
48 blue pairs Goldschild linen Nel 50/3
1 white pair Goldschild linen Nel 50/3
1 gimp pair Goldschild linen Nel 30/3

Conch
48 blue pairs Goldschild linen Nel 50/3
1 white pair Goldschild linen Nel 50/3
1½ gimp pairs Goldschild linen Nel 30/3

Crab
50 blue pairs Goldschild linen Nel 50/3
10 white pairs Goldschild linen Nel 50/3

Starfish
50 blue pairs Goldschild linen Nel 50/3
2 white pairs Goldschild linen Nel 50/3

Instructions:
Prickings
A black and white copy of the diagram was reduced in size to make the pricking.
Set on and work as shown in the diagram. The markings on the conch and the cockle are made using a twisted gimp or a few stitches of embroidery, or a combination of both. Add an extra twist to the ground stitch.

To make up:
When you have worked all the doilies, cut through the middle of the plaits marked „A", to separate them. Fold along the row of twists between B and C, tuck the plaited ends out of sight and stitch along the edge.

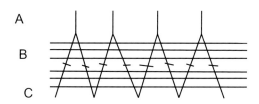

The finishing touch:
You can embroider markings on the conch and the cockle, using contour stitches or couching, to add a finishing touch.

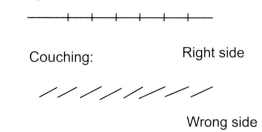

Couching: Right side

                              Wrong side

Couching: Bring your needle up on the left and down on the right to lay a thread over the lace, then make small stitches over the top, from right to left. See diagram.

Contour stitches
                              Right side

Contour stitches:
A row of stitches worked close together. Make the first stitch on the diagonal, start the second half way along it. See diagram.

Never ending doilies

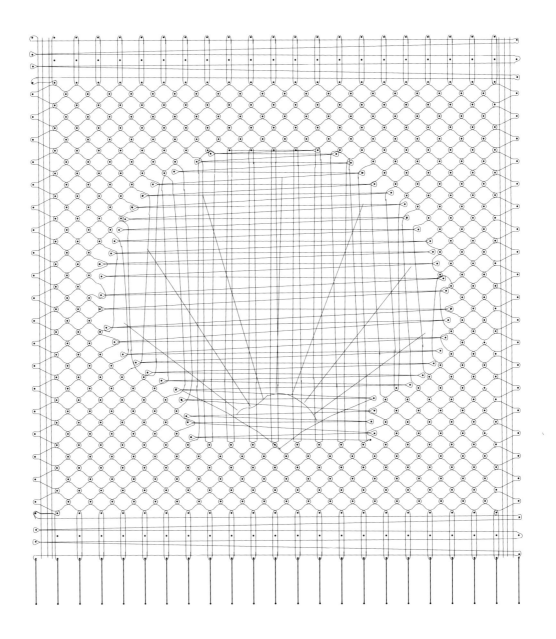

Never ending doilies

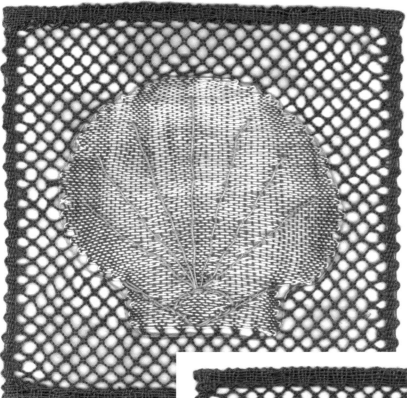

Never ending doilies
Cockle

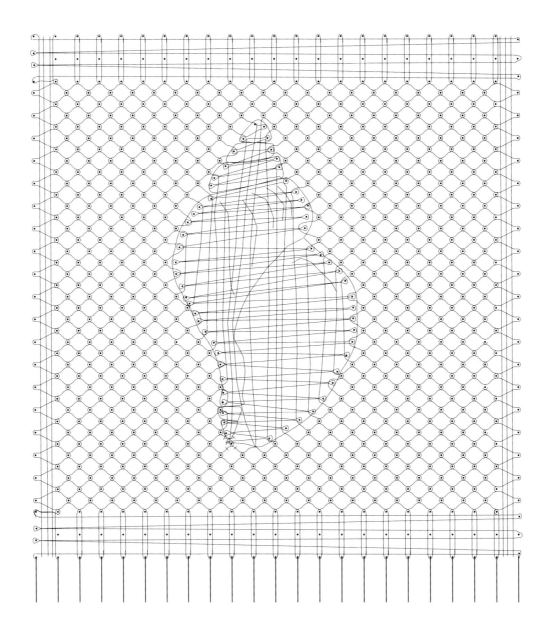

Conch

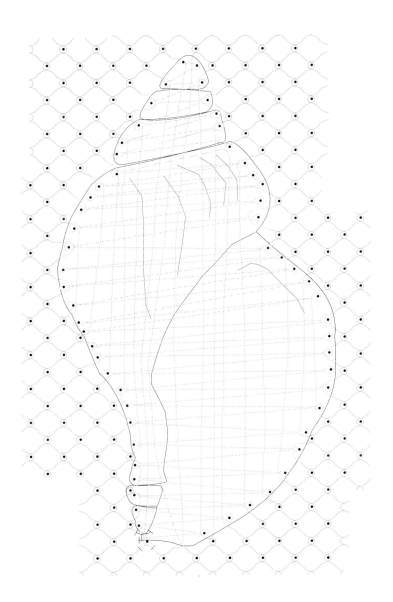

Cockle

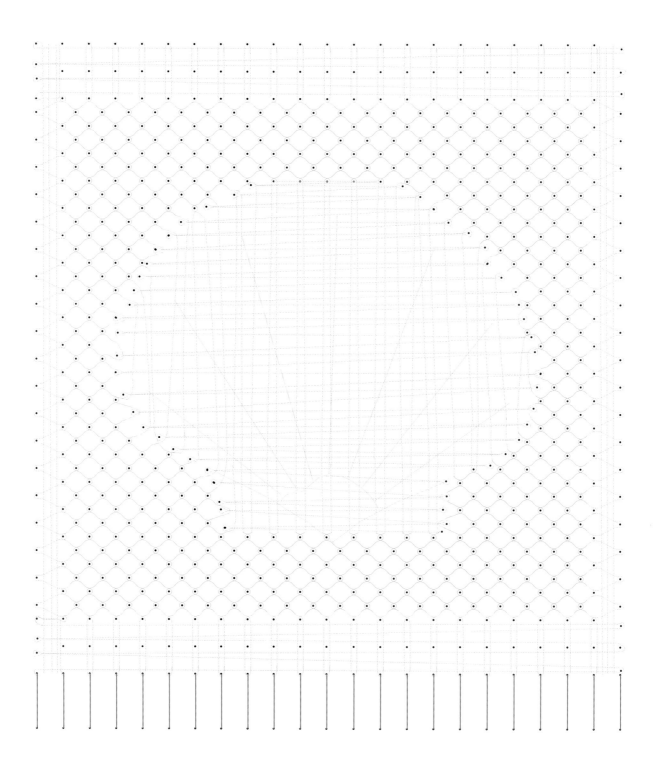

Never ending doilies

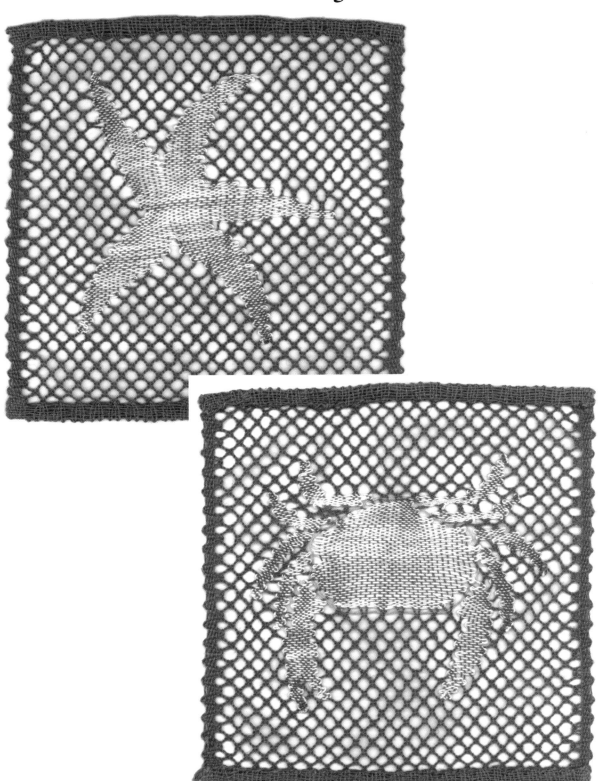

Never ending doilies
Starfish

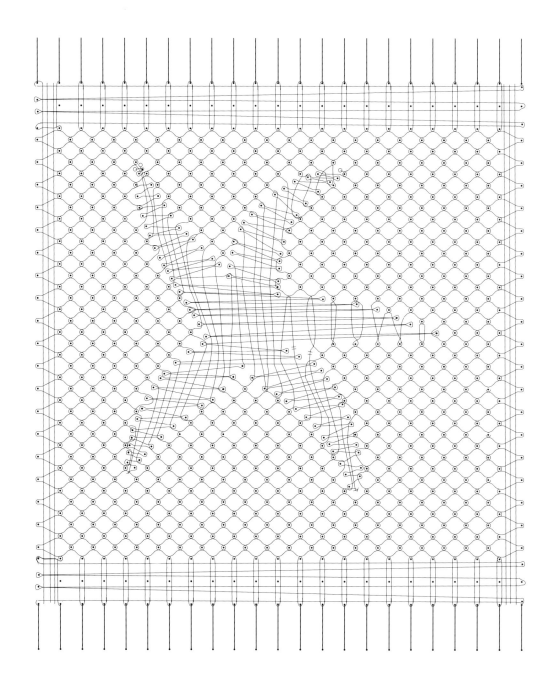

Starfish

Never ending doilies
Crab

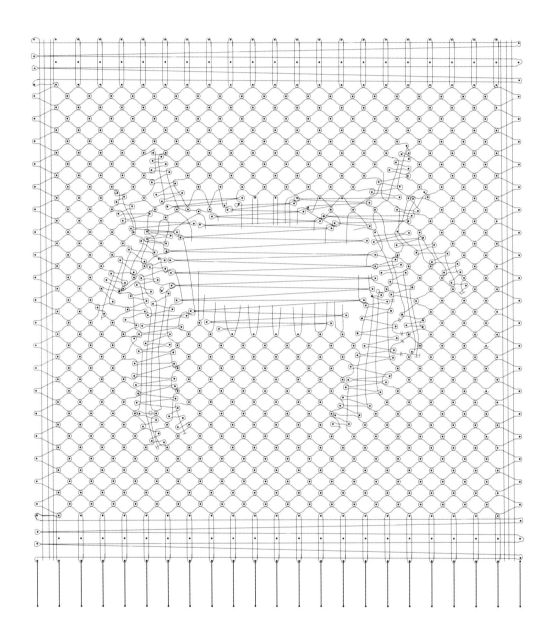

Crab

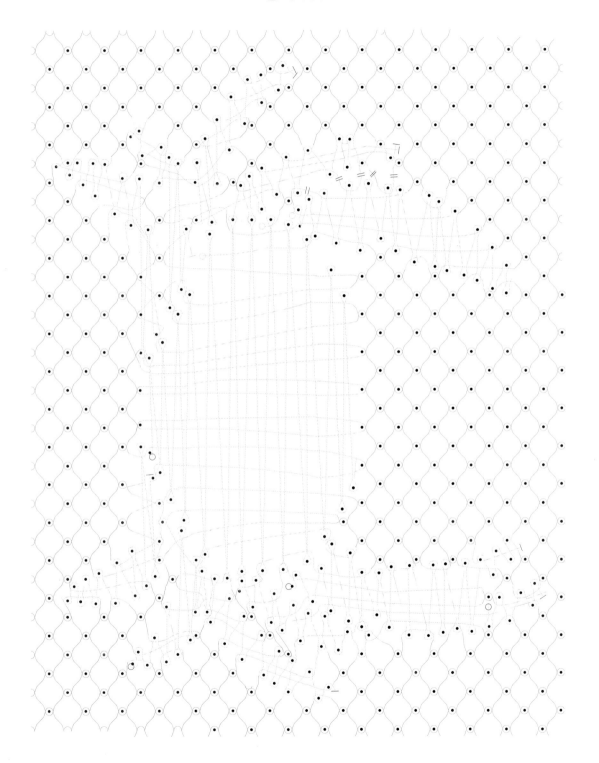

"The Lighthouse"

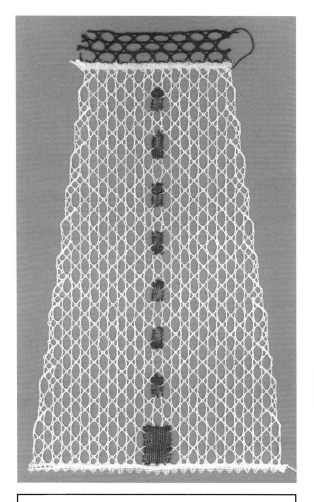

Picture of the finished lighthouse.

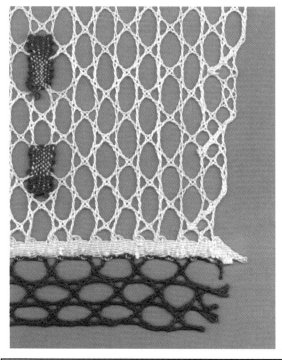

Close up of where you work the banister and finish off the lighthouse at the same time.

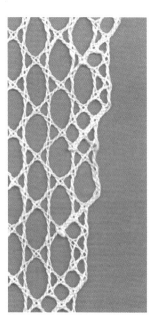

Close up of how you take out the pairs at both sides.

"The Lighthouse"

Materials:

Goldschild linen Nel 50/3
Lower edge: 4-5 white pairs
Tower: 56 white pairs and 1 red pair *
Banister: 7 red pairs and 2-3 white pairs
Light: 12 yellow pairs
Roof: 16 black pairs

Instructions:

Wind the red pair with a lot of thread on one bobbin and just enough on the other bobbin to work the door or the window. When that section is complete, cut off the pair and wind off thread from the full bobbin, ready to work the next window.

Start working the narrow cloth tape at the bottom of the lighthouse. Add 2 new pairs at every pin on the right (see fig. 1), ready to work the lighthouse. To work the door, add the red pair as workers. (See *).

The lighthouse gradually becomes narrower by working as follows: the blue marks on the diagram show where 2 pairs are worked as one, half stitch, pin, half stitch. Plait towards the next pin. Take the 2 pairs from the plait as a single pair to work a cloth stitch. Plait towards the next pin. Take the 2 pairs from the plait as a single pair to work a cloth stitch. Plait towards the next pin. Throw out one bobbin from each pair and continue (fig. 2).

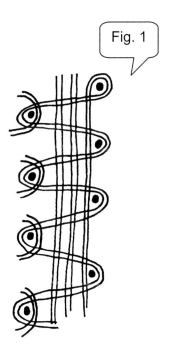

Fig. 1

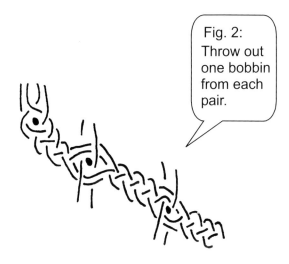

Fig. 2: Throw out one bobbin from each pair.

For the window surround, see fig. 3. The windows are cloth stitch with red workers. Use the pinholes which are close together. See the picture on page 40.

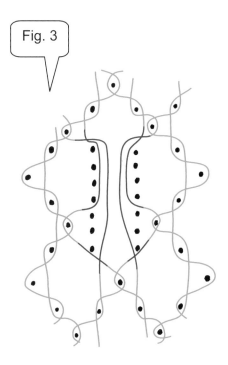

Fig. 3

The roof starts with 6 pairs, adding in one pair at each side until you have 16 pairs. To add in, work cloth stitch and twist, pin, hang a new pair on the pin, one thread over and one under the inner pair. Close with a cloth stitch and twist, and continue in half stitch. See fig. 5.

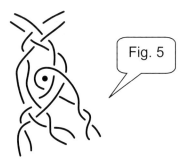

Fig. 5

The banister is worked at the same times as the lighthouse is finished off (fig. 4).

To leave out pairs at the corresponding pins, work a cloth stitch, pin, lay back the inner pair, close with a cloth stitch and twist and continue in half stitch. Tie off the pairs you laid back, see fig. 6.

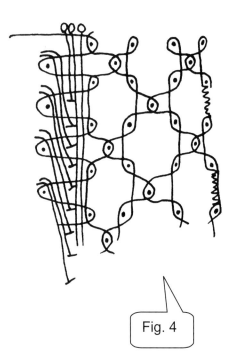

Fig. 4

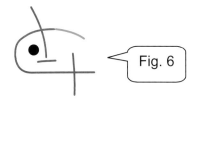

Fig. 6

"The Lighthouse" (top)

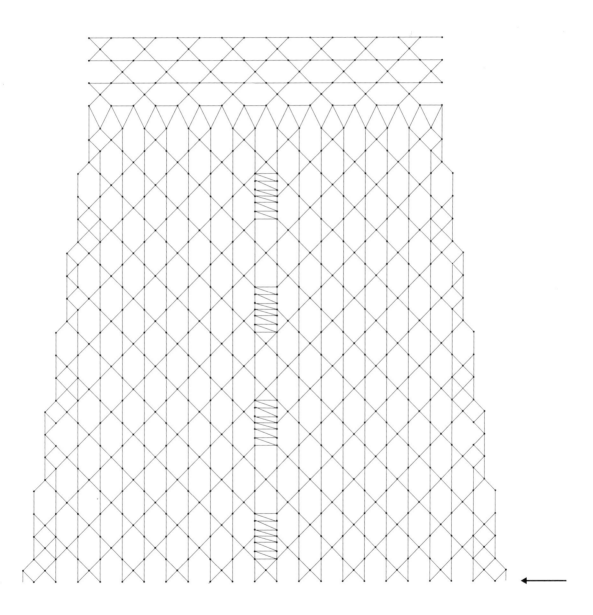

"The Lighthouse" (bottom)

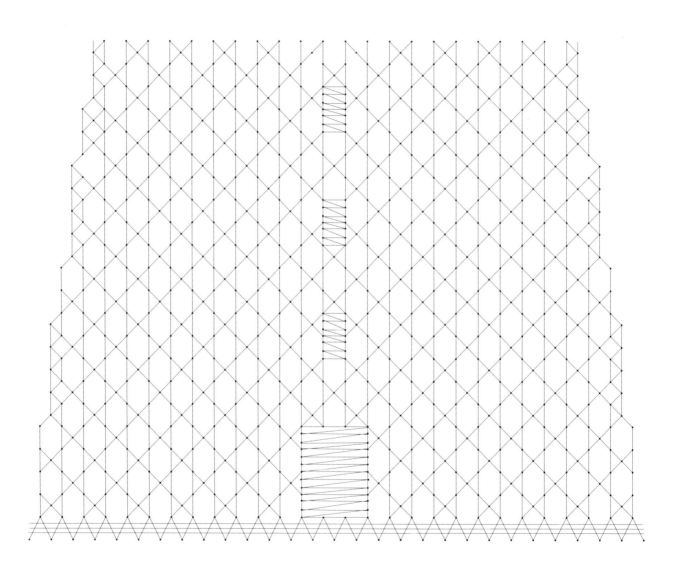

"The Lighthouse"

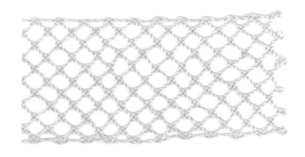

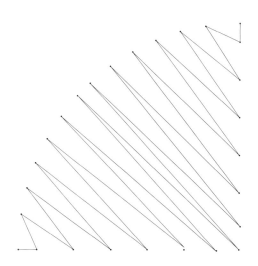

"The Lighthouse"

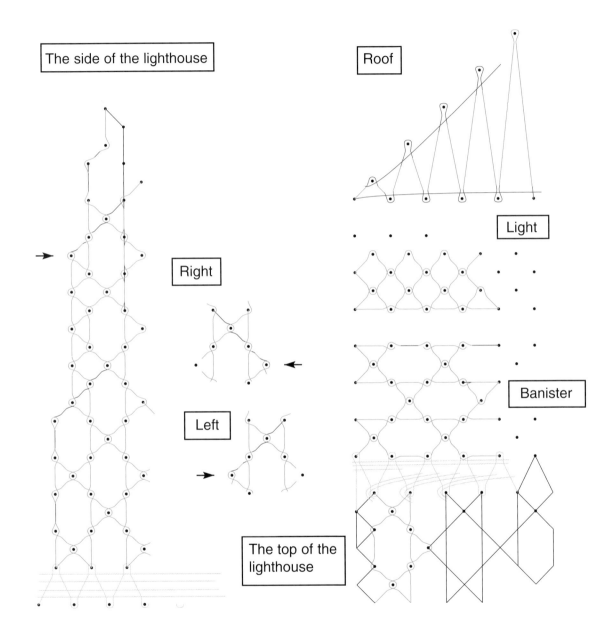

The side of the lighthouse

Roof

Right

Left

Light

Banister

The top of the lighthouse

The sea with a ship

Materials:
Aprox. 48 blue pairs Goldschild linen Nel 50/3
3 white pairs Goldschild linen Nel 50/3

Instructions:
Start at the dotted line on the pricking, or where you find appropriate. Follow the diagram and work 1 to 4 ships, as you wish.

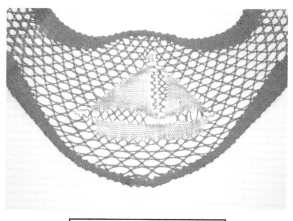

Close up of the ship.

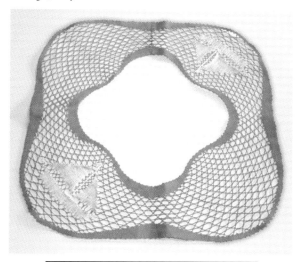

Photo of the finished lace, showing two ships.

General info:
On the following pages you will find diagrams and prickings for the sea and the ship. You will need the middle section and two small side segments to make up one quarter of the pricking.

Pricking / diagram:
I have not drawn in all the passive pairs for the cloth stitch, in the diagram, just given a rough idea of how many pairs to use.

The sea with a ship

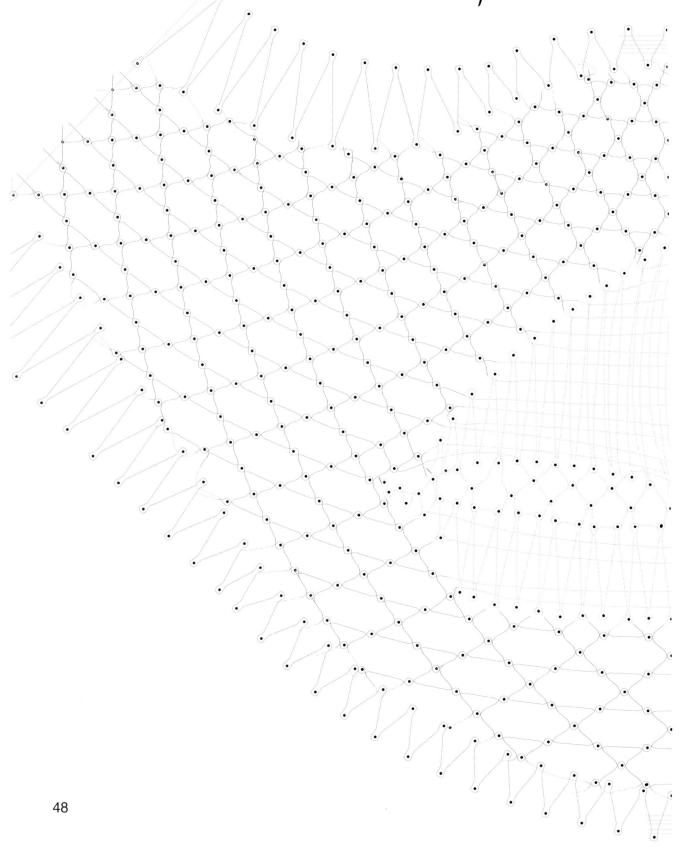

The sea with a ship

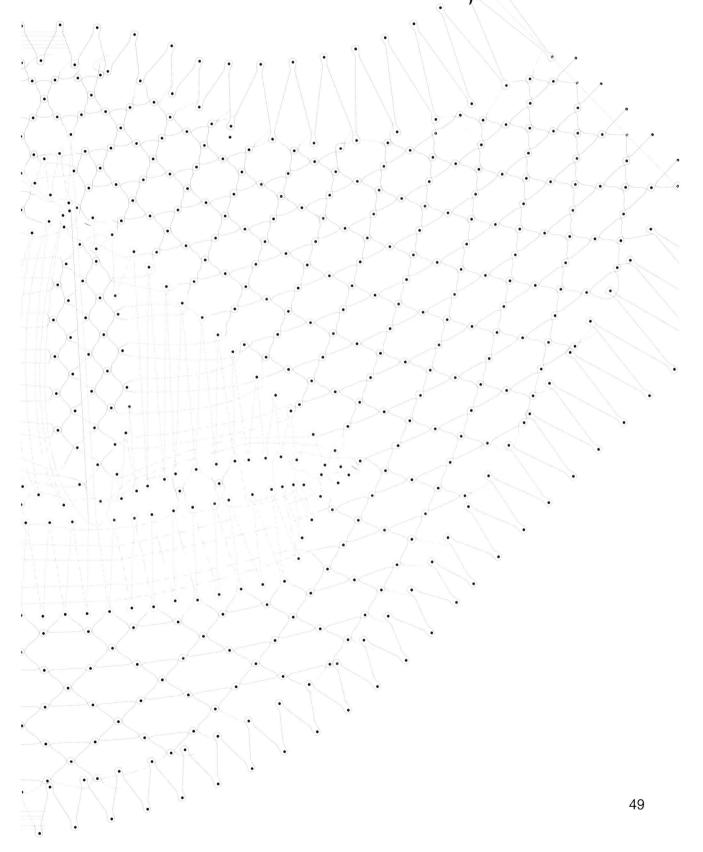

The sea with a ship

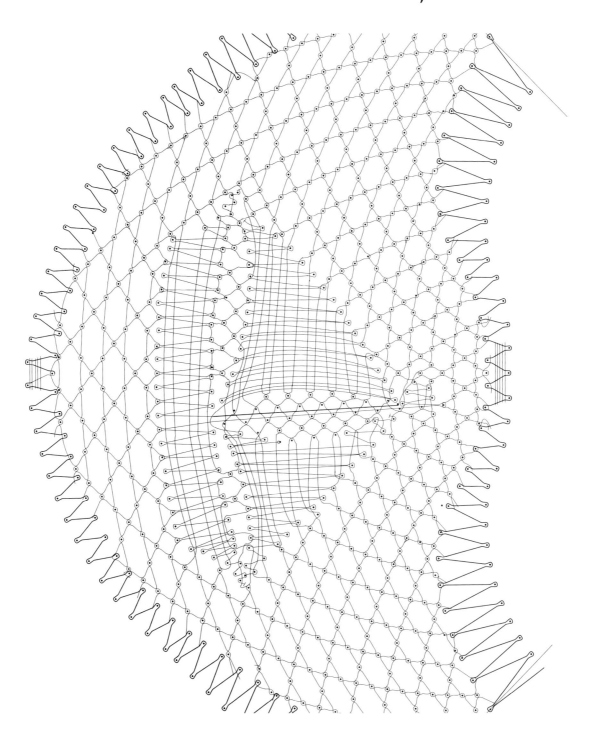

The sea with a ship / The sea without a ship

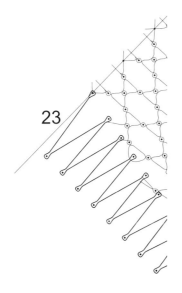

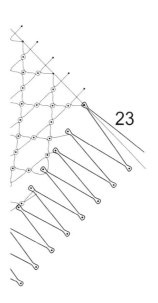

The sea without a ship

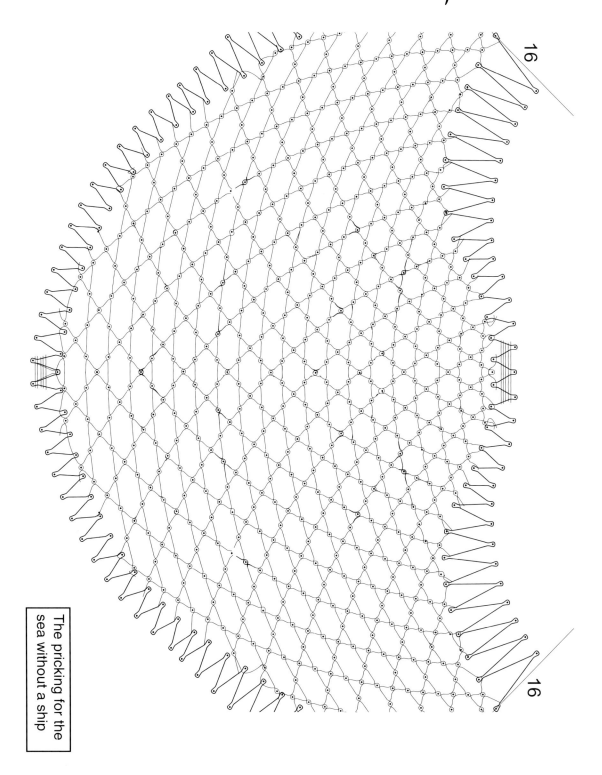

16

16

The pricking for the sea without a ship

Ufo "Marguerite"

Materials:

4 yellow pairs Goldschild Nel 50/3 for the inner ring
5 white pairs and 1 yellow pair Goldschild Nel 50/3 for the outer ring

Instructions:

You can work this all in one go, or work the inner ring first and the outer ring later. Set on and work as shown in the diagram. The inner ring is worked in cloth stitch with yellow thread. The outer ring is worked in cloth stitch with white passives and a yellow worker pair, which becomes the edge pair by working the stitch shown in fig. 1. The white pairs work in half stitch, then cloth stitch and twist with the yellow pair at the edge.

To finish:

Sew out and finish with a row of knots. (See p.79.)

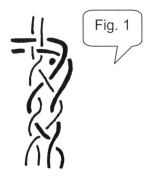

Fig. 1

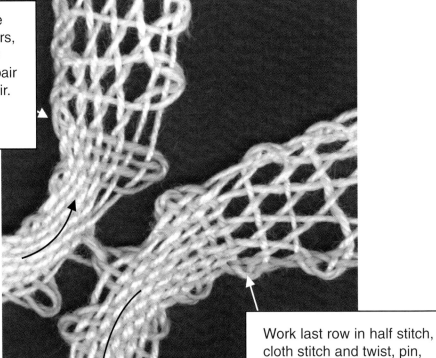

Cloth stitch across the row with yellow workers, twist them, pin, CTTC (fig 1), so the yellow pair becomes the edge pair.

Work last row in half stitch, cloth stitch and twist, pin, CTTC (fig. 1), then the yellow pair become the workers.

Ufo "Marguerite"

Ufo "Marguerite"

The line marks
the start.

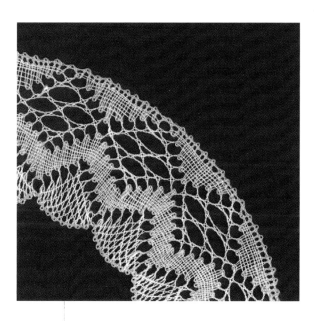

Mirror edge

Materials:
17 white pairs Goldschild Nel 50/3
3 yellow pairs Goldschild Nel 50/3

Instructions:
Set on and follow the diagram. Add 3 yellow pairs where indicated by the arrows.

To finish:
Finish off by sewing out and knotting off, as shown on page 79, or any other method you prefer.

Worked by Fanny Nielsen

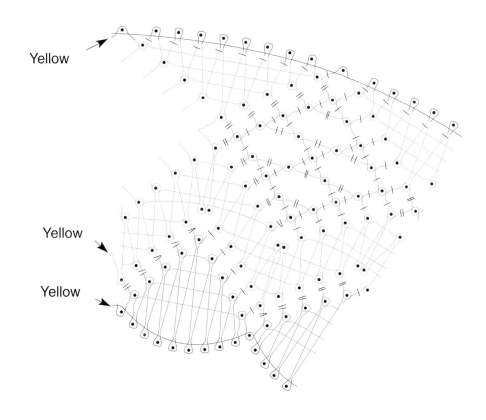

Yellow

Yellow

Yellow

Mirror edge

Square Glass Coasters "Roseground"

Materials:
12 white pairs Goldschild Nel 50/3
3 yellow pairs Goldschild Nel 50/3

Instructions:
Set on and work as shown in the diagram. Add
the yellow pairs as indicated by the arrows.
The yellow thread will follow the trail shown on
the pricking with a bold line.

To finish:
Sew out and tie off.

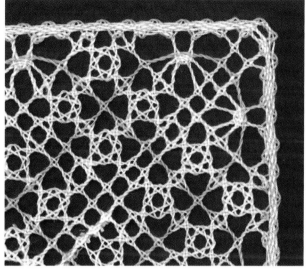

"The Window"

Materials:
13 white pairs Goldschild Nel 50/3
2 yellow pairs Goldschild Nel 50/3

Instructions:
Set on and work as shown in the diagram. The
yellow worker pairs are added where shown by
the arrows.

To finish:
Sew out and tie off.

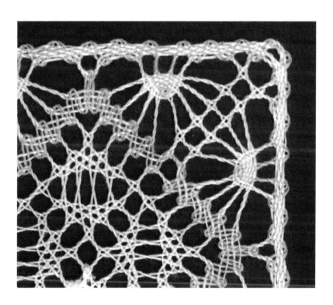

Square Glasscoaster "Roseground"

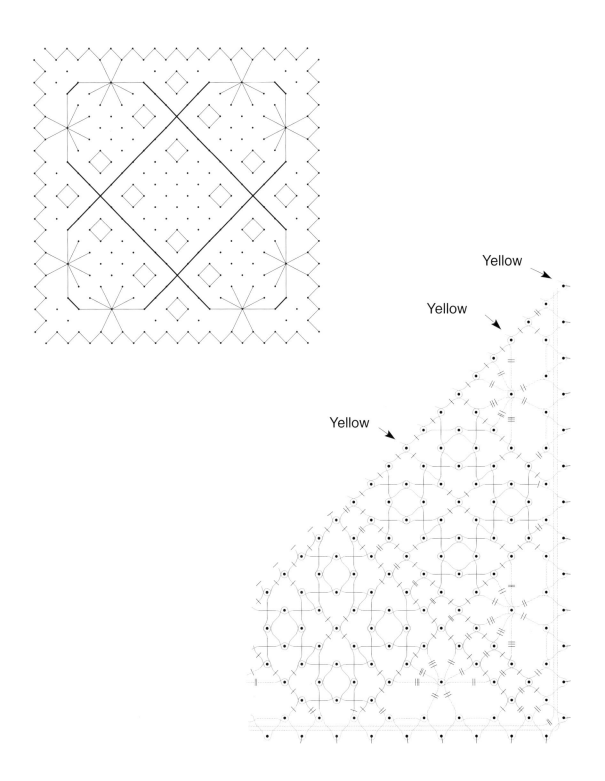

Yellow

Yellow

Yellow

Square Glasscoaster "The Window"

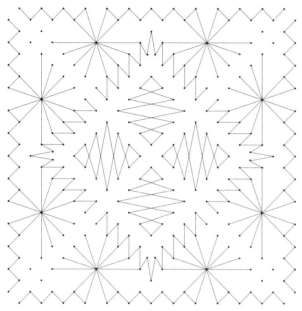

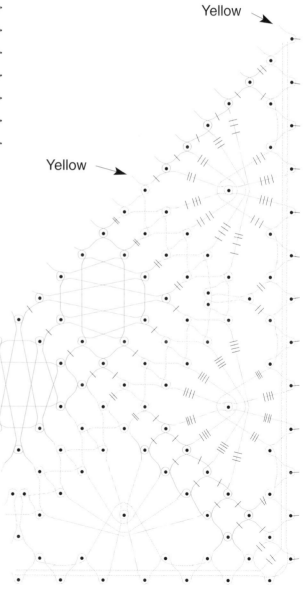

Yellow

Yellow

61

A flower with round petals

Materials:

7 pairs Goldschild linen Nel 80/3 for each of the small and medium sized flowers, 9 pairs for the large one. Use one (or more) pairs with a sparkly thread and add beads if you wish.

Instructions:

Start with cloth stitch and follow the diagram. Add the sparkly thread at x, where it will be the worker thread in half stitch. To keep the sparkly thread in place, make sure it is lying in the correct position after the edge stitch, i.e. as the 4th bobbin after a cloth stitch and twist on the left side, or as the first after a cloth stitch and twist on the right. Each time you work the stitch at the end of a row, add an extra twist to keep the sparkly thread in place.

N.B. In some situations you may find the sparkly thread in the wrong place. Correct it by using this stitch at the edge: Cross – twist – twist left pair – cross – twist (see fig. 1).

Add beads to look like dew drops on the petals. Put a hook through the hole in a bead, draw the thread through to make a loop and take the partner bobbin through the loop. See fig. 2. Pull the bobbins apart to slide the bead up into position.

The workers and left pair from the plait meet with a C – T – T – C, see fig. 3. You may need an extra twist on the worker to get the sparkly thread back in the right place.

Inside the point of the flower petal, use the pinhole several times by making a scroll. (See p.79.)

The pair at the edge next to the pivot pin is twisted 3 times, and becomes the scroll pair. *Work towards the pivot pin as usual. Instead of working with the scroll pair, pass the workers over them, round the back of the pin and under the scroll-pair. Work back across the row. Repeat from * several times to complete the scroll. The scroll pair reverts to being the edge pair. When you have sewn into the pin below the pivot, remove the pivot pin and pull each pair carefully into position.

To finish:

Each part of the flower can be starched and held in shape until it is dry. The layers are then stitched together in the middle, adding a bead for decoration.

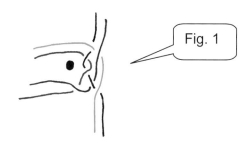

Fig. 1

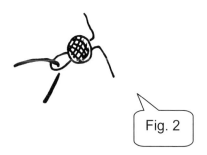

Fig. 2

A flower with round petals

Fig. 3

Middle set of petals.

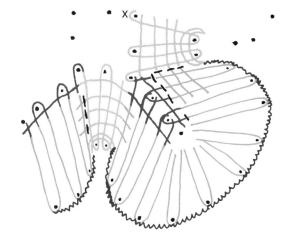

Diagram for the smallest and middle sets of petals.

The 2 inner layers of the flower.

Smallest set of petals.

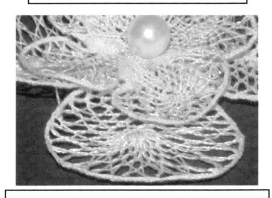

Close up of the 2 inner layers.

A flower with round petals

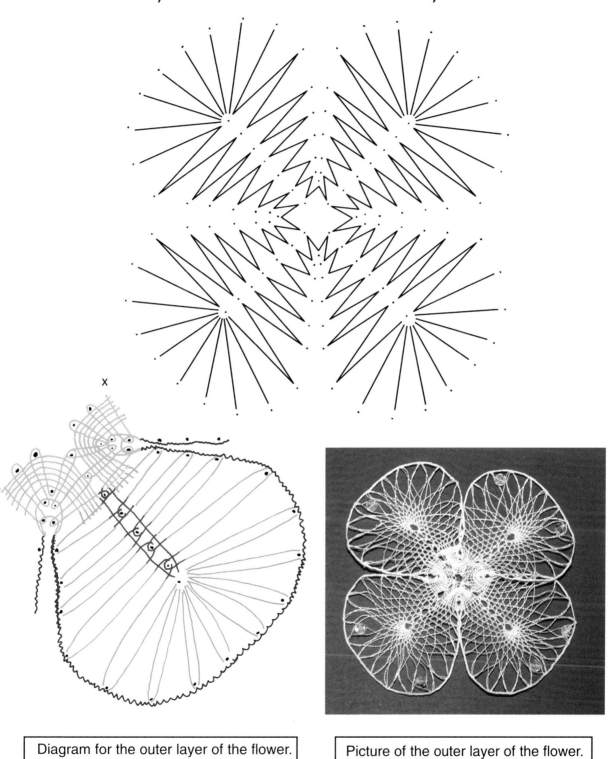

x

| Diagram for the outer layer of the flower. | Picture of the outer layer of the flower. |

A flower with pointed petals

Materials:

7 pairs Goldschild linen Nel 80/3 for each parts of theflower. Use one (or more) pairs with a sparkly thread and add beads if you wish.

Start with cloth stitch and follow the diagram. Add the sparkly thread at x, where it will be the worker thread in half stitch. To keep the sparkly thread in place, make sure it is in the correct position after the edge stitch, i.e. as the 4th bobbin after a cloth stitch and twist on the left side, or as the first after a cloth stitch and twist on the right. Each time you finish the stitch at the end of a row, add an extra twist to leave the sparkly thread in the right place.

N.B. In some situations you may find the sparkly thread in the wrong place. Correct it by using this stitch at the edge: Cross – twist – twist left pair – cross – twist (see fig. 1).

Add beads to look like dew drops on the petals. Put a hook through the hole in a bead, draw the thread through to make a loop and take the partner bobbin through the loop. See fig. 2. Pull the bobbins apart to slide the bead up into position.

The workers and left pair from the plait meet with a C – T – T – C, see fig. 3. You may need an extra twist on the worker to get the sparkly thread back in the right place.

Inside the point of the flower petal, use the pinhole several times by making a scroll. (See the techniques page, 79.)

The pair at the edge next to the pivot pin is twisted 3 times, and becomes the scroll pair. *Work towards the pivot pin as usual. Instead of working with the scroll pair, pass the workers over them, round the back of the pin and under the scroll-pair. Work back

across the row. Repeat from * several times to complete the scroll. The scroll pair reverts to being the edge pair. When you have sewn into the pin below the pivot, remove the pivot pin and pull each pair carefully into position.

To finish:

Each part of the flower can be starched and held in shape until it is dry. The layers are stitched together in the middle, adding a bead for decoration.

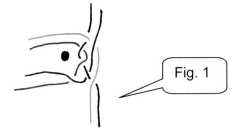

Fig. 1

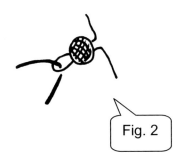

Fig. 2

A flower with pointed petals

Smallest set of petals.

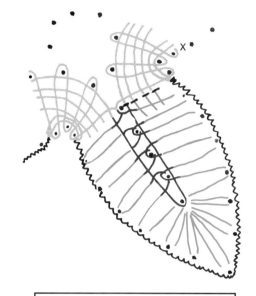

Diagram for the smallest and largest set of petals.

Middle set of petals.

Close up of the 2 inner layers of the flower.

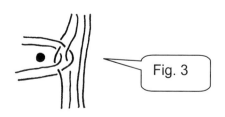

Fig. 3

A flower with pointed petals

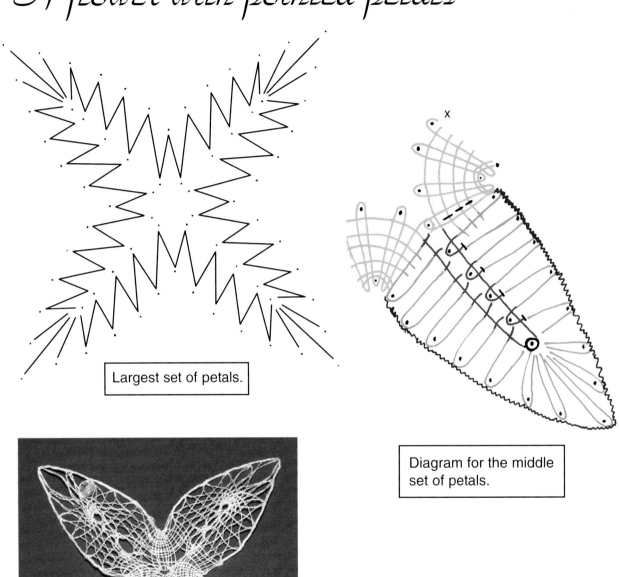

Largest set of petals.

x

Diagram for the middle set of petals.

Runner and Doily „Zigzag"

Runner:

Materials:

54 pairs Ground colour Goldschild Linen Nel 30/3
2 light pairs Goldschild Linen Nel 30/3
6 dark pairs double thread Goldschild Linen Nel 30/3 as a gimp

Instructions:

Start with open pairs along the diagonal line between part 1 and 2. Finish part 1 (in the direction of the arrow) and work parts 2 and 3 simultaneously, following the direction of the arrows. The row of pinholes indicated by the arrows is printed on both sections of the pricking, so they must overlap.

To finish:

Finish as you began.

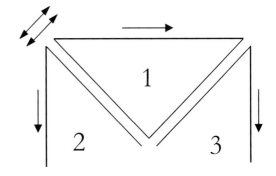

This drawing shows where to start and which direction to work the runner.

Doily:

Materials:

21 ground colour pairs Goldschild Linen Nel 30/3
1 light pair Goldschild Linen Nel 30/3
2 dark pairs double thread Goldschild Linen Nel 30/3 as a gimp.

Instructions:

Start by working along the diagonal and follow the diagram all the way round.

To finish:

Finish along the start line. Sew out and tie off.

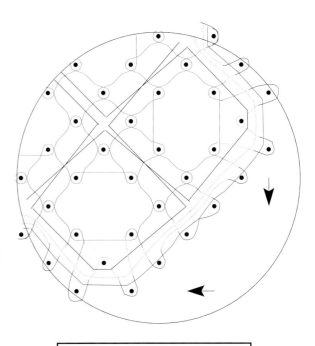

Detail drawing of the corner of the runner and the doily.

Runner and Doily „Zigzag"

72

73

Doily „Zigzag"

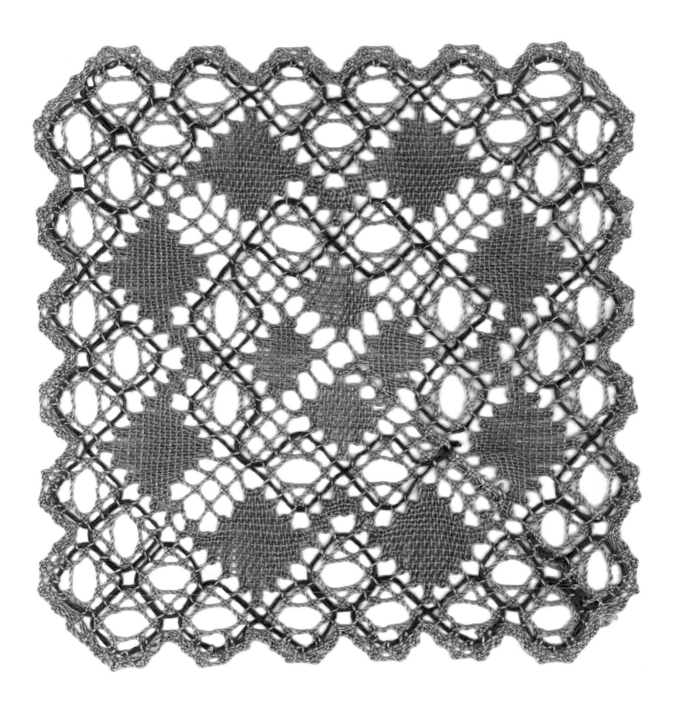

Doily „Zigzag"

Doily „Zigzag"

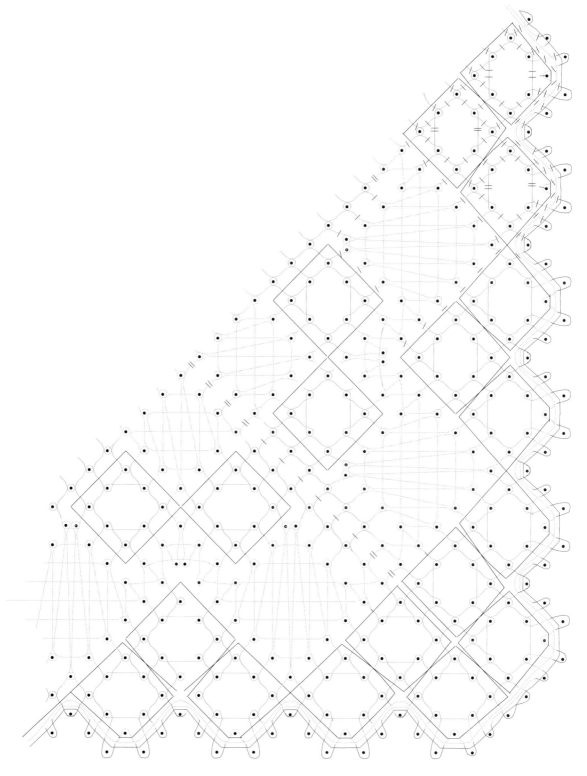

Colour Code

Red ——————————————————— Cloth stitch with a twist (CTCT)

Green ——————————————————— Half stitch (CT)

Purple ——————————————————— Cloth stitch (CTC)

Blue ——————————————————— Cloth stitch (CTC)

Blue zig zag ——————————————————— Plait (TC)

Black ——————————————————— Twist (T)

Black ——————————————————— Gimp

Pattern Markings

⊙———— Add a pair

⊢ Take out a pair

/\/\/\/\/\/\/\ Plaiting

√ Sew in / out

Techniques

Scroll – using the same pin 3 times or more

Set the pin and twist the pair closest to it three times (scroll-pair). * Work towards the pivot pin. Instead of working with the scroll pair, pass the workers over them, round the back of the pin and under the scroll pair. Work back across the row. Repeat from * several times to complete the scroll. The scroll pair reverts to being the edge pair. When you have worked the pin below the pivot, remove the pivot pin and pull each pair carefully into position.

Tying off

When tying off with knots, you work a series of knots, across the row and back again. Start opposite the workers with a reef knot.
From left to right:
• Make a simple knot (half knot) by passing the first bobbin (left) over the second bobbin (right). Pull tight.
• The first bobbin goes to the right of and under the second bobbin and is laid to one side. The second bobbin becomes „first bobbin." Continue to the end of the row and finish with a reef knot.
From right to left:
• Make a simple knot (half knot) by passing the first bobbin (right) over the second bobbin (left). Pull tight.
• The first bobbin goes to the left of and under the second bobbin and is laid to one side. The second bobbin is now „first bobbin." Continue to the end of the row and finish with a reef knot.
Cut all threads off closely.

Linen finish (Straight finish in cloth stitch)

Start on the left side with the workers. *Work 3 cloth stitches, lay the workers to the back of the lace. Start on the left again with the pair at the left side as workers. *. Repeat from * to * until there are 3 pairs remaining. Make a plait with these 3 pairs and stitch to the back of the lace.

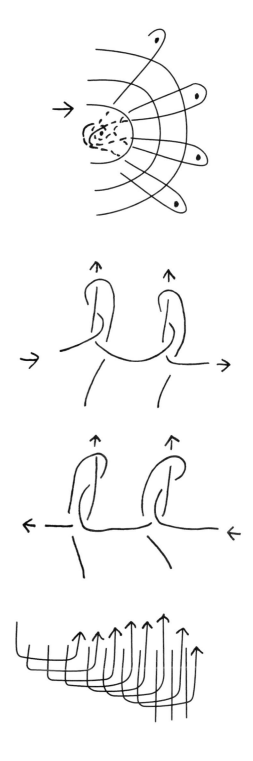

Supplier

Goldschild linen threads can, together with other lace items, be bought from:

Knipleshoppen på Bogø

V/ Birgit Poulsen
Bogø Hovedgade 107 B
DK-4793 Bogø By
Denmark
Tel. / fax (+ 45) 5589 3605

Mail order.
Visitors welcome by appointment.